7⃝ MEALS one

TRIP TO THE STORE

Shop Smart.
Cook Smart.

.

BY KELLY DONLEA

Wishing you cooking Success!

Ky Donlea

Contents

Introduction

The Challenge

For many, an extremely challenging part of the day is dinnertime. It is the largest meal of the day and falls at the busiest time. Even if they cook often, many people don't feel that they have the right tools and strategies to make a hot, healthy meal for their families night after night.

We are here to help! Welcome to the first cookbook that approaches "dinner" from a lifetime perspective. Not one night at a time, or with a **weekly** script, we give you the strategies for a lifetime of success. Using our simple guidelines, you will **never** have to make an extra trip to the store for dinner again. This book teaches how to **shop smart** and stock up on ingredients that lead to dinner success.

The Solution

The solution is here. Our inexpensive shopping lists are streamlined to include only the most multitasking ingredients we could find that will enable you to make any one of the wide variety of recipes in this book — any night of the year — with what you have at home. We call these "Smart Ingredients"

Every other cookbook gives you ingredients lists recipe by recipe resulting in new ingredients each night, and a cabinet full of "ingredient" clutter. This book gives you ingredients lists that can be used to make any recipe in this book. That's right, 70 meals!

The reality is that families today are busier than ever and dinner often becomes and afterthought. Let us help you make dinner easy and a success, even if it is an afterthought.

Our Goal

at Organizing Dinner is to provide you with solutions for success at dinnertime, every night — even if you have no idea what to make a half hour before dinnertime. 70 Meals, One Trip to the Store will help you bridge the gap between meal planning (or lack thereof) and cooking the meals your family loves, with a lifetime plan for success.

How It Works

Step 1: Semiannual Shopping Trip (for Smart Ingredients)

To start, stock up on the Smart Ingredients in the Semiannual List. As the name implies, this list only needs to be replenished twice a year. Don't be intimidated: we thoroughly researched ingredients for their multitasking ability and streamlined each and every recipe in ths book to only use ingredients that are used by many others. You will be surprised at how little you have to buy, and how much money you save, when you cut out the "ingredient clutter".

Step 2: Weekly Shopping List

The incredibly easy second step is to add the 14 ingredients on the weekly list to your grocery list.

Step 3: Cook!

You will simplify your kitchen life, and best of all... organize dinner. When 4 p.m. rolls around you will never again feel the sense of panic over dinner. You will turn to the Recipe Index have everything **on hand** to make **any one** of these meals in the book, and check an important "To Do" off your list.

> ### SMART INGREDIENT TIP
>
> *Most of the ingredients on the Semiannual List are dry. And the 3 meat bases can be frozen. You can make dinner for weeks by simply making a quick weekly stop for milk, butter, cheese and bread.*

Shopping Lists

The 70 recipes in this book include pizza, pasta and soups in addition to several recipes based on ground beef, chicken breasts and white fish fillets. These are three of the most versatile meats, and allow for a variety of recipes.

After stocking your pantry with the Smart Ingredients on the Semiannual List, you can start to successfully make dinner every night with the help of the short, 14-item Weekly List, or even get by, if you choose, by just buying milk, butter, eggs and bread. Talk about a cheap meal plan! The lists are organized into categories to make your shopping even easier. Also, some items leave room for personal preference. For example, the Weekly List includes "Bread item". Buy what your family prefers, and tailor your recipe to that, i.e. if your family prefers pita bread to rolls, use that instead. No one (in this cookbook especially) said that chicken sandwiches have to be eaten on a certain type of roll. The goal is to make dinner work for you.

You may need to restock on some particular ingredients sooner that twice a year, but you can trust that they will be few and they will be ingredients you can use in many other recipes in this book.

Printable versions of the Semiannual and Weekly Shopping Lists are available on our website at www.organizingdinner.com

SMART INGREDIENT TIP

Fresh vs. Packaged: Using fresh produce is always the better way to go. But having canned or frozen varieties on hand is also a lifesaver when it comes to making dinner. Buy what you know you will use, or buy both and maximize your trip to the store. Use fresh vegetables first, and know you have a supply of canned and frozen Smart Ingredients to ensure you always have what you need to make a variety of dinners.

Semiannual Shopping List

Quantities are general, and are based on cooking for 4 people. If you will be cooking for larger or smaller groups, adjust the quantities accordingly.

CANNED GOODS

- [ ] Canned tomato soup, 3 - 10.5 oz. cans
- [ ] Canned diced tomatoes, 12 – 14 oz. cans
- [ ] Chicken broth, either 8 – 14 oz. cans or packaged bouillon to make your own broth
- [ ] Canned or dry black beans, 6 - 15 oz. cans, or equivalent
- [ ] Canned cream of mushroom soup, 6 – 10.5 oz. cans
- [ ] Canned mushrooms, 6 – 4 oz. cans
- [ ] Canned marinated artichoke hearts, 2 - 4 oz. cans
- [ ] Tomato paste – 8 - 6 oz. cans

CONDIMENTS

- [ ] Soy Sauce, 10 oz.
- [ ] Olive oil, 1 liter
- [ ] Vegetable oil, 1 liter
- [ ] Jar of diced garlic, 12 oz. (or add fresh garlic to your weekly list if you prefer)
- [ ] Balsamic vinegar, 10 oz.
- [ ] Worcestershire sauce, 12 oz.
- [ ] Dijon mustard, 8 oz.
- [ ] Hot sauce, 8 oz. (Buy a sauce that suits your "heat" preference. There are mild hot sauces that will still add the required flavor).
- [ ] Bottled lemon juice, 8 oz.

DRY GOODS

- [ ] Rice, 5 lb. bag
- [ ] Flour, 5 lb. bag
- [ ] Yeast, 4 oz. jar
- [ ] Corn bread mix, 2 packages
- [ ] Pasta: 4 lbs. spaghetti noodles, 3 lbs. rotini, macaroni or other thick noodles
- [ ] Salt, 8 oz.
- [ ] Pepper, 4 oz.
- [ ] Garlic salt, 4 oz.
- [ ] Italian Seasoning (this is a spice combination), 4 oz.
- [ ] Taco seasoning, 6 oz.
- [ ] Bread crumbs, 10 oz. canister
- [ ] Parmesan cheese, 2- 10 oz. cannisters
- [ ] Honey, 8 oz. jar
- [ ] Powdered Italian dressing mix – 6 single serving packets
- [ ] Chopped pecans, 8 oz.

FREEZER AISLE

- [ ] Frozen spinach, 2 - 10 oz. packages
- [ ] Frozen mixed vegetables (mixture of peas, carrots, etc.) 2 - 2 lb. bags
- [ ] 2 packages of 2-crust pie crusts

Weekly Shopping List

PRODUCE

Purchase quantities based on what you plan to use for the week. If you aren't sure you will use the produce in recipes, you can always cut and serve it with, or as, a side salad.

☐ 3 Onions
☐ 2 Green bell peppers
☐ Lettuce, your preference, equivalent to 1 head
☐ 1 Tomato

BUTCHER

☐ Ground beef, 2 lbs. *As a general guideline, 85% lean ground beef is the most versatile. It is inexpensive, contains great flavor, and holds its shape nicer than some of the leaner ground meats. Feel free to substitute other ground meat, but when using ground poultry or pork, cook at a slightly lower temperature. Ground meat can be frozen for up to 3 months. Defrost in the refrigerator overnight, or in the microwave.*

☐ 8 Fish fillets   *Orange roughy, tilapia and halibut are the most versatile; salmon or or other fish filets can also be used.*

☐ 8 boneless skinless chicken breasts

DAIRY

☐ Eggs, 1 dozen
☐ Butter, 1 package, equivalent to 2 cups
☐ Milk   *Your preference (the skimmer the milk, the thinner the creaminess of the recipes). If you don't drink milk in your household, you can opt to take milk off your weekly list, and add canned condensed milk to your Semiannual Shopping List. Dilute with an equal amount of water for the quantity called for in the recipe i.e. if the recipe calls for 1 cup of milk, use ½ cup water and ½ cup condensed milk.*
☐ Shredded Mozzarella cheese, 16 oz.
☐ Shredded Monterey jack/cheddar cheese blend, 16 oz.

BAKERY

☐ Bread item, (1 loaf of bread, or 8 rolls, 8 pita, etc.)
☐ Tortillas, 8 large

Organizing Dinner
Tips & Tricks

Following are some tips and tricks that help any kitchen become more organized and help you win the game at dinnertime:

1 Get rid of the clutter. Throw away ingredients you have not used in 6 months to a year. Box up the kitchen gadgets and rarely-used equipment and move it out of the kitchen.

2 Placement. Only leave the most useful kitchen tools in the cooking "Zone" (this is the area you occupy during your prep and cooking time). Everything else goes into the outer cabinets or storage. This can also help you get rid of some tools you may discover you don't use. When what you most use is organized in the Zone, prep time and clean up becomes quick and easy.

3 Keep a plastic grocery bag on or around the counter while you prepare. All the garbage goes into this bag. It keeps you organized and saves you from going back and forth to the garbage can.

4 Put away as you go. With most meals there are lulls during the cooking process while things simmer or bake. Put away the ingredients you've already used during this time/ shove a few of the prep dishes into the dishwasher/ clean off the counter where you're done prepping. When your Smart Ingredients are also in the Zone, this becomes super easy.

5 Approach dinner as a sport. Gear up with good equipment, show up ready to play and give yourself credit for a win. And remember, you get better with practice!

SMART INGREDIENT FACT

One of our favorite Smart Ingredients, canned diced tomatoes, is reputed as the canned product that most retains its nutritional value compared to its fresh counterpart. Also, when you use canned tomatoes, you are actually getting more lycopene in your diet because of the concentration of the product.

Recipe Index

CHICKEN RECIPES   pages 18-40

Recipe Index

GROUND BEEF RECIPES   pages 42-61

Recipe Index

Recipe Index

PASTA, SOUPS & MORE   pages 80-95

Chicken Recipes

1

Pecan-Crusted Chicken

INGREDIENTS

4 chicken breasts
½ teaspoon salt
¼ cup honey
⅓ cup butter, softened
2 tablespoons Dijon mustard
1 cup bread crumbs
½ cup finely chopped pecans

Preheat oven to 350° F. Pound and trim chicken breasts. Season with salt. Combine honey, butter and mustard in a small bowl; stir well. Combine bread crumbs and pecans in shallow dish and stir well. Baste chicken first in honey mixture, and then in pecan/bread crumb mixture. Place chicken in baking dish. Drizzle with remaining honey mixture. Bake, uncovered, for 35 minutes.

Italian-Style Chicken with Spinach and Tomatoes

INGREDIENTS

4 chicken breasts
2 tablespoons olive oil
1 teaspoon diced garlic
½ onion, diced
1 can diced tomatoes
½ package frozen spinach, thawed
1 teaspoon Italian seasoning
2 tablespoons balsamic vinegar
8 oz. spaghetti noodles
4 tablespoons Parmesan cheese

Cook spaghetti according to package directions. Meanwhile sauté onions and garlic in oil for 2 minutes until lightly browned. Add chicken, balsamic vinegar and Italian seasoning and cook over medium high heat in frying pan about 5 minutes each side. Add diced tomatoes and spinach to the pan. Cook until fully heated and some liquid evaporates. Serve over pasta, and top each serving with 1 tablespoon Parmesan cheese.

Grecian Chicken

INGREDIENTS

4 chicken breasts
1 tablespoon olive oil
1 can marinated artichoke hearts
1 can diced tomatoes
1 teaspoon Italian seasoning
2 cups rice

Cook rice according to package directions. Heat oven to 300 ° F. Heat oil in frying pan over high heat. Add chicken seasoned with Italian seasoning and cook until just browned on both sides, but not cooked through. Add artichoke hearts, tomatoes with their liquids, and chicken to Dutch oven or large oven-safe pot. Cook uncovered in oven for 60 minutes. Serve over rice.

This dish may also be cooked in a crock pot for at least 3, and up to 8 hours.

4

Creamy Crock Pot Chicken

INGREDIENTS

3 chicken breasts, cubed
2 tablespoons butter
One can cream of mushroom soup
1 ½ cups water
¼ onion, diced
1 cup dry rice or noodles

Add first five ingredients to crock pot. Simmer for at least 3 hours, and up to 8 hours. Add rice or noodles during last half hour of cooking. Stir occasionally during this time, and add more water 1/8 of a cup at a time if needed for desired consistency.

5

Chicken Pot Pie

INGREDIENTS

2-3 chicken breasts, diced
2 tablespoons, and ⅓ cup butter
¼ onion, diced
⅓ cup flour
⅓ cup milk
½ teaspoon salt
¼ teaspoon pepper
14 oz. chicken broth
2 cups mixed vegetables, thawed
1 package 2-crust pie crust

Cook chicken in 2 tablespoons butter on stove until cooked through.
Set one pie crust in bottom of pie dish. In large saucepan melt 1/3 cup
butter over medium heat. Add onion. Cook 2 minutes, stirring frequently
until tender. Stir in flour, salt and pepper until well blended (have liquids
on hand during this step). Gradually stir in broth and milk stirring until
bubbly and thickened. Stir in chicken and mixed vegetables. Remove from
heat and add mixture to pie pan. Top with second crust and seal edge.
Cut slits in top of pie crust. Bake at 400 ° F for 50 minutes. Let stand
for 10 minutes prior to cutting.

Chicken Parmesan

INGREDIENTS

4 chicken breasts
3 tablespoons olive oil
2 cups Mozzarella cheese
1 egg, whisked
1 cup bread crumbs
¼ cup Parmesan cheese
1 tablespoon Italian seasoning
¼ teaspoon salt
¼ teaspoon black pepper

1 onion, chopped
1 teaspoon diced garlic
1 can diced tomatoes
1 can tomato paste
1 tablespoon hot sauce
2 tablespoons balsamic vinegar
1 teaspoon sugar
½ cup water
1 lb. Spaghetti or other thick noodles

Heat 1 tablespoon oil in deep pot on stove over medium-high heat. Add onion and garlic, stirring for 5 minutes until soft. Add tomatoes with juices, tomato paste, balsamic vinegar, Italian seasoning, hot sauce, sugar and water. Reduce heat to low, and simmer 30 minutes, stirring occasionally. Meanwhile, heat 1 tablespoon olive oil in deep pan on medium-high heat. Combine bread crumbs, salt, pepper and 1/8 cup Parmesan cheese. Baste chicken in egg and then bread crumb mixture. Cook chicken in batches in oil 8 minutes each until browned well on all sides. To a baking dish, add sauce and then chicken. Top with Mozzarella cheese. Bake, uncovered, at 350°F for 20 minutes or until cheese is melted and lightly browned. Meanwhile cook noodles in separate pot according to package directions. Serve chicken and sauce over noodles. Top with remaining Parmesan cheese.

Chicken Stir-Fry

INGREDIENTS

4 chicken breasts, cut into strips
1 onion, cut into strips
1 green pepper, cut into strips
1 tablespoon vegetable oil
¼ cup soy sauce
1 teaspoon diced garlic
2 cups rice

Cook rice according to package directions. Heat oil in wok or frying pan on high. Add garlic, onion and green pepper. Stir constantly for 5 minutes. Add chicken. Continue stirring, and when chicken is nearly cooked through, add soy sauce. Cook one minute more. Serve over rice.

Chicken Fajitas

INGREDIENTS

4 chicken breasts cut into strips
½ cup vegetable oil
1 package Italian dressing mix
1 teaspoon taco seasoning
2 green peppers, cut into strips
1 onion, cut into strips
1 cup shredded cheddar/jack cheese
1 cup lettuce, shredded
8 tortillas
1 tablespoon lemon juice

Place chicken in Ziploc bag with Italian dressing packet, all but 2 tablespoons oil, and taco seasoning. Marinate chicken at least one half hour in refrigerator. Cook chicken and vegetables over high heat in frying pan, stirring constantly until browned. Sprinkle with lemon juice. Serve on tortillas and garnish with cheese and lettuce.

Parmesan-Crusted Baked Chicken

INGREDIENTS

1 cup Parmesan cheese
2 teaspoons Italian seasoning
¼ cup butter, melted
4 chicken breasts
1 teaspoon salt
½ teaspoon pepper

Combine Parmesan cheese, Italian seasoning, salt and pepper. Line shallow baking pan with foil. In small pan on stove, or bowl in microwave, melt butter until just melted, not boiling. Baste chicken breasts in butter, then in cheese mixture and place on foil-lined pan. Bake, uncovered, at 350°F for 35 minutes or until completely cooked.

Chicken Stroganoff

INGREDIENTS

3 tablespoons butter
1 teaspoon diced garlic
4 chicken breasts, cut into strips
½ medium onion, diced
1 can mushrooms
1 can diced tomatoes
1 can cream of mushroom soup
1 lb. thick noodles

Sauté garlic, mushrooms and onion in butter in pan on stove over medium heat for 5 minutes. Add chicken and stir until cooked through. Add soup and diced tomatoes with some of their juices. Stir well and simmer until thickened. Meanwhile cook noodles according to package directions. Spoon chicken mixture over pasta and serve.

This dish can also be cooked inthe crock pot. If doing so, add all ingredients, except noodles, and cook at least 3, and up to 8 hours. Include all liquid from tomatoes. Add noodles, and water if needed, during last ½ hour of cooking.

Buffalo Chicken Sandwiches

INGREDIENTS

4 chicken breasts
½ cup hot sauce
2 tablespoons olive oil
1 cup flour
1 teaspoon garlic salt
¼ teaspoon black pepper
½ cup butter
4 rolls
4 slices lettuce
4 slices onion

For Buffalo Sauce, heat butter and hot sauce in a small pan on stove just until butter melts; turn heat to low, cover and keep warm on stove top. Combine flour, garlic salt and pepper. Coat chicken well in the flour mixture. Heat oil in large skillet, and cook chicken breasts for approximately 15 minutes, turning once or twice until browned and cooked through. Drain chicken briefly, then immediately toss in buffalo sauce mixture and remove. Serve on rolls with lettuce and onion.

Classic Fried Chicken

INGREDIENTS

4 chicken breasts
1 cup oil
1 cup flour
1 teaspoon salt
1 teaspoon pepper
½ teaspoon of hot sauce

Pound chicken breasts until tender. Cut into smaller pieces if desired. Brush chicken breasts with hot sauce. Heat oil in deep skillet or large heavy pot. Shake remaining ingredients in paper bag. Drop chicken breast in bag individually, and shake to coat. Fry in oil approximately 15 minutes, turning once or twice until browned and cooked through.

13

Chicken Cacciatore

INGREDIENTS

4 chicken breasts
¼ cup olive oil
1 onion, chopped
1 green pepper, chopped
2 teaspoons garlic, diced
2 tablespoons balsamic vinegar
1 teaspoon Italian seasoning
1 can diced tomatoes
2 cups rice

Cook rice according to package directions. In frying pan, heat oil and sauté onion, garlic and pepper. Transfer veggies to a small bowl with a slotted spoon leaving oil in pan. Add chicken and sauté until lightly browned. Drain fat from pan and add to it vinegar, Italian seasoning and tomatoes with juices. Return chicken and veggies to pan, cover and sauté on low for 20 minutes. Serve over rice.

Chicken Fried Rice

INGREDIENTS

2 chicken breasts, diced
⅓ cup oil
4 tablespoons soy sauce
1 cup rice, uncooked
2 ½ cups chicken broth
2 cups onion, coarsely chopped
¼ cup green pepper, finely chopped
2 eggs, slightly beaten
1 cup lettuce, finely shredded

Cook chicken in 1 tablespoon oil in hot skillet, stirring constantly until lightly browned. Set chicken aside in bowl, and add to it 1 tablespoon soy sauce. Stir. Add remainder of oil and rice to skillet. Reduce heat to medium. Stir frequently until golden brown. Add chicken with soy sauce and broth. Simmer, covered, for 25 minutes or until rice is tender. Stir in onion, green pepper, and remaining soy sauce. Cook, uncovered, over medium heat until liquid is absorbed. Push rice mixture to side of skillet, and add eggs. Stir eggs until they are almost set, then add lettuce and continue stirring for another minute. Blend with rice.

Lemon Honey Chicken

INGREDIENTS

4 chicken breasts
1 teaspoon salt
½ teaspoon pepper
½ cup butter, melted
3 tablespoons lemon juice
½ cup honey

Season chicken with salt and pepper. Combine melted butter, lemon juice and honey. Using half the lemon/honey mixture, marinate chicken for at least one half hour. Grill or bake chicken, basting frequently with remaining lemon/honey mixture. If baking, line baking dish with foil and bake for 40 minutes at 350° F.

Barbecue Chicken

INGREDIENTS

4 chicken breasts
2 cups barbecue sauce (see recipe below)

BARBECUE SAUCE

1 can tomato paste
¼ onion, chopped
3 teaspoons sugar
1 tablespoon butter
1 tablespoon Dijon mustard
1 teaspoon soy sauce
1 teaspoon garlic salt
1 teaspoon hot sauce

For barbecue sauce, combine all ingredients and cook over medium heat until onion is tender and sauce thickens. Remove from heat. Cool. Marinate chicken in one half of barbecue sauce for at least 20 minutes. Discard marinade. Grill over medium heat for 8 minutes until chicken is cooked through, basting with remaining sauce near end of cooking time.

Sweet and Savory Chicken with Lemon Pepper Salsa

INGREDIENTS

¼ cup diced green pepper
¼ cup chopped onions
3 tablespoons lemon juice
1 teaspoon hot sauce
1 teaspoon garlic, minced
4 chicken breasts
2 tablespoons soy sauce
2 teaspoons oil
2 tablespoons honey
2 cups rice
salt and pepper

For salsa, mix green pepper, onions, 2 tablespoons lemon juice, hot sauce and garlic in small bowl to blend. Season to taste with salt and pepper. Cover and refrigerate.

Season chicken with salt and pepper. Whisk soy sauce and oil in medium bowl to blend. Add chicken and stir to coat. Marinate in refrigerator for at least one half hour. Whisk honey and remaining 1 tablespoon lemon juice in another small bowl. Grill chicken over medium-high heat until cooked through, brushing occasionally with honey glaze, about 6 minutes per side. Meanwhile cook rice according to package directions. Serve chicken with salsa mixture over rice.

Chicken Caesar Wraps

INGREDIENTS

3 chicken breasts, diced
⅓ cup olive oil
1 egg
½ teaspoon salt
¼ teaspoon pepper
1 teaspoon garlic, mashed
¼ cup Parmesan cheese
1 teaspoon lemon juice
4 tortillas
2 cups lettuce, diced

Cook chicken in 1 tablespoon oil over medium heat, stirring frequently until cooked through. Let cool. For dressing, whisk together egg, remaining oil, salt, pepper, garlic, Parmesan cheese and lemon juice. Add chicken to dressing mixture and toss to coat. Spoon ¼ mixture onto each of 4 tortillas, and add equal amounts of lettuce. Roll to form wraps.

Chicken Enchiladas

INGREDIENTS

1 can tomato paste
3 tablespoons vegetable oil
2 teaspoons taco seasoning
1 teaspoon hot sauce
2 teaspoons flour
1½ cups water
1 teaspoon garlic salt
4 chicken breasts, cut into strips
4 cups chicken broth
1 teaspoon garlic, minced
½ onion, diced
1 tomato, diced
8 tortillas
1 ¼ cups shredded cheddar/jack cheese

For sauce, combine tomato paste, oil, taco seasoning, hot sauce, flour, water, and garlic salt in pan on stove. Bring to boil; simmer 5 minutes.

In large pot on stove, combine chicken, broth and garlic. Bring to boil. Reduce heat to medium-low and simmer about 1 hour. Strain chicken, run cold water over it and shred into a bowl. Mix in tomatoes and onions. Place equal amounts of chicken and 1/8 cup cheese in center of each tortilla, roll up and place in pan, seam side down. Sprinkle with remaining cheese. Ladle on enough sauce to cover, then add remaining ¼ cup cheese. Bake at 425° F for 20 minutes. Serve with remaining sauce on the side.

Chicken and Black Bean Quesadillas

INGREDIENTS

8 tortillas
3 chicken breasts, cut into thin strips
1 cup shredded cheddar/jack cheese
½ can black beans, rinsed and drained
½ tomato, diced
¼ onion, diced
½ packet Italian Dressing mix
1 tablespoon taco seasoning
3 tablespoons olive oil

Combine chicken, oil, Italian dressing mix and taco seasoning, and marinate for at least one half hour. Cook chicken in frying pan over medium high heat, stirring frequently until cooked through, about 7 minutes. Spread equal amounts of chicken and beans over 4 tortillas. Top with cheese and cover with remaining 4 tortillas. Cook each quesadilla in frying pan on one side until cheese is melted enough to hold everything together. Flip in pan and warm on other side. Slide onto plate, and cut into 6 wedges. Serve with diced tomatoes and onion.

Once assembled, quesadillas can also be cooked in microwave. Place on microwave plate, cook on high for 1 minute each.

Chicken and Black Bean Chili

INGREDIENTS

3 chicken breasts
3 cups chicken broth
2 tablespoons taco seasoning
1 can black beans, rinsed and drained
1 can diced tomatoes with juices
1 can tomato paste
½ teaspoon salt
1 tablespoon oil
½ onion, diced
½ green pepper, diced
2 tablespoons hot sauce

In large pot on stove, combine chicken, broth and taco seasoning. Bring to boil. Reduce heat to medium-low and simmer until chicken is falling apart, about 1 ½ hours. Meanwhile, sauté onion and pepper in oil until slightly soft, about 5 minutes. When chicken is done simmering, add vegetables and all remaining ingredients to pot. Stir, and continue cooking over medium heat until thickened.

Chicken Strata

INGREDIENTS

6 slices of bread, or equivalent, cubed
2 chicken breasts, cubed
4 tablespoons butter
1 can mushrooms
1 cup cheddar/jack OR Mozzarella cheese
⅓ cup Parmesan cheese
1 diced fresh tomato or 1 can diced tomatoes, drained
3 eggs, beaten
1 cup milk
1 teaspoon salt
1 teaspoon pepper

Line bottom of a 13 x 9 x 2" buttered baking dish with bread. Top with chopped chicken. In a small frying pan, melt 2 tablespoons of the butter over medium heat. Add mushrooms and saute until browned, 3 to 5 minutes. Remove from heat and add to baking dish. Top with both kinds of cheese and tomatoes. In a large bowl, combine milk, eggs, salt and pepper. Mix until well blended. Pour over chicken. Bake, uncovered, at 350°F for 50 minutes.

Ground Beef Recipes

23

Meatball Sandwiches

INGREDIENTS

2 slices bread, crumbled
⅓ cup milk
1 egg
¼ cup Parmesan cheese
1 tablespoon Italian seasoning
¾ teaspoon garlic salt
¼ teaspoon black pepper
1 lb. ground beef
¼ cup olive oil

1 onion, chopped
1 can diced tomatoes
1 can tomato paste
1 tablespoon balsamic vinegar
1 teaspoon honey
1 tablespoon hot sauce
½ cup water
1 cup Mozzarella cheese
4 rolls

Soak bread in milk until softened. Add egg, Parmesan cheese, 1/2 tablespoon Italian seasoning, garlic salt and pepper. Stir. Add ground beef, and using a teaspoon, form into 16 small meatballs. Heat oil in deep skillet. Cook in batches for 8 minutes, turning frequently until browned well on all sides. Remove meatballs from skillet. Discard all but 2 tablespoons fat from skillet. Add onion and cook, stirring often, until softened. Add tomatoes, tomato paste, 1 tablespoon balsamic vinegar, honey, remaining Italian seasoning, hot sauce and water. Reduce heat to low, and simmer 25 minutes. Return meatballs to skillet and cook, uncovered 15 minutes. Dish 4 meatballs onto each of 4 rolls. Spoon sauce over. Top each with ¼ cup Mozzarella cheese. Toast if desired.

Spaghetti and Meatballs

INGREDIENTS

2 slices bread, crumbled
⅓ cup milk
1 egg
¼ cup Parmesan cheese
1 tablespoon Italian seasoning
¾ teaspoon garlic salt
¼ teaspoon black pepper
1 lb. ground beef
¼ cup olive oil

1 medium onion, chopped
1 can diced tomatoes
1 can tomato paste
1 tablespoon balsamic vinegar
1 teaspoon honey
1 tablespoon hot sauce
½ cup water
8 ounces of spaghetti noodles

Soak bread in milk until softened. Add egg, Parmesan cheese, ½ tablespoon Italian seasoning, garlic salt and pepper. Stir. Add ground beef, and using a tablespoon, form into approximately 8 meatballs. Heat oil in skillet. Add meatballs and cook over medium-high heat, turning often until browned all over, approximately 8 minutes. Remove meatballs from skillet. Discard all but 2 tablespoons fat from skillet. Add onion and cook, stirring often, until softened. Add tomatoes, tomato paste, balsamic vinegar, honey, remaining Italian seasoning, hot sauce and water. Reduce heat to low, and simmer 25 minutes. Return meatballs to skillet and cook, uncovered 15 minutes.

Meanwhile cook spaghetti in separate pot according to package directions. Serve meatballs and sauce directly over noodles. Top with additional Parmesan cheese if desired.

Tomato Soup Meatballs with Rice

INGREDIENTS

2 cups rice
1 can condensed tomato soup
1 can diced tomatoes, drained
1 small onion, minced
1 teaspoon garlic, diced
¼ cup bread crumbs
1 egg
1 teaspoon Italian seasoning
¼ teaspoon salt
¼ teaspoon pepper
1 lb. ground beef
1 tablespoon oil
¾ cup milk

Cook rice according to package directions. Combine ¼ cup condensed soup, tomatoes, onion, garlic, bread crumbs, egg, Italian seasoning, salt and pepper. Add beef and mix well. Form into meatballs. Heat oil in skillet. Add meatballs and cook over medium high heat, turning often until browned all over, about 8 minutes. Add remaining soup, milk and diced tomatoes. Bring to a boil, reduce heat to low, cover and simmer until meatballs are cooked through, about 15 minutes. Serve meatballs and sauce over rice.

Traditional Meatloaf

INGREDIENTS

1 lb. ground beef
½ can cream mushroom soup
¼ onion, diced
1 teaspoon Worcestershire sauce
½ teaspoon garlic salt
½ cup bread crumbs
¼ cup grated Parmesan cheese
¼ teaspoon pepper
1 can tomato paste

Mix all ingredients except tomato paste by hand and form into a loaf in shallow pan. Bake, uncovered, 1 hour at 350° F. Spread tomato paste over loaf during last 10 minutes of cooking.

Italian Meatloaf

INGREDIENTS

1 lb. ground beef
1 can diced tomatoes
½ cup bread crumbs
1 egg
½ teaspoon salt
½ teaspoon hot sauce
½ cup Mozzarella cheese
½ medium onion, diced
¾ teaspoon Italian seasoning

Mix all ingredients by hand and form into loaf into shallow pan.
Bake, uncovered, about 1 hour at 350° F.

28

Honey Mustard-Glazed Meatloaf

INGREDIENTS

1 lb. ground beef
⅓ cup bread crumbs
2 eggs
½ cup chopped onion
1 teaspoon Italian seasoning
½ teaspoon salt
¼ teaspoon pepper
3 tablespoons Dijon mustard
3 tablespoons honey

Mix first 7 ingredients by hand and form into a loaf in shallow pan. Combine honey and mustard, brush half of the mixture on loaf. Bake at 350° F for 30 minutes. Brush with remaining honey and mustard mixture. Bake, uncovered for 30 to 45 minutes longer.

Kitchen Sink Meatloaf

Let's face it, there are recipes for meatloaf whose ingredients include everything but the kitchen sink. There are meatloaf recipes that include bacon, cheddar cheese, broccoli, and many other ingredients. So we've created our own version of the Kitchen Sink, using ingredients you will already have at home. There are so many ways you could change this recipe; feel free to experiment and make it your own.

INGREDIENTS

1 lb. ground beef
1 can diced tomatoes, drained
½ cup bread crumbs
1 egg
½ teaspoon salt
½ teaspoon pepper
1 teaspoon Worcestershire sauce
½ teaspoon hot sauce
½ cup cheddar/jack cheese
¼ cup Parmesan cheese
½ onion, diced
½ green pepper, diced
1 can tomato paste

Form all ingredients except tomato paste into loaf. Bake, uncovered, about one hour at 350° F. Spread tomato paste on top of loaf during last 10 minutes of cooking.

Delicious Hamburgers

Hamburgers are a meal that can literally be made with just one ingredient: ground beef. Renowned, award winning chef James Beard's recipe calls for nothing more than a little butter on either side of a lightly formed patty of ground beef seasoned with salt and pepper. We recommend adding a little Worcestershire sauce for flavor, and foregoing the added fat in the butter. But the point here is, this is another extremely flexible meal. Form your ground beef into 4 patties with one egg or 1/2 cup breadcrumbs if that suits your fancy, or else, prepare simply as below.

INGREDIENTS

1 lb. ground beef
salt and pepper to taste
1 tablespoon Worcestershire sauce
4 rolls

Season beef with salt, pepper and Worcestershire sauce, and form into four round patties. Grill over medium-high heat for 6 minutes, turning once. Top with cheese, onions, tomatoes and lettuce as desired.

Pizza Burgers

INGREDIENTS

1 lbs. ground beef
½ cup Mozzarella cheese
3 tablespoons oil
4 tablespoons flour
4 tablespoons water
½ medium bell pepper, diced
1 medium onion, diced
1 can tomato paste
1 can diced tomatoes
2 cups rice
salt and pepper

Form beef into 8 thin hamburger patties (two patties will make one hamburger). Place equal amounts of cheese in the middle of four patties. Place remaining patties on top of the cheese filled patty. Knead together edges to form four large patties. In large skillet, add oil; brown hamburger patties on both sides, place on paper towels to drain. Using the oil in the pan, make a thick brown gravy by aggressively whisking in flour and water by tablespoonfuls until a runny gravy is achieved. Add tomato paste, diced tomatoes, chopped onion and green pepper, and salt and pepper to taste. Stir well and simmer for approximately 10 minutes. Return hamburgers to sauce, cover and cook on low heat for approximately 20 minutes, stirring frequently. Meanwhile, cook rice according to package directions. Place one hamburger on each serving of rice, cover with sauce mixture.

Beef Dumpling Soup

INGREDIENTS

½ onion, diced
2 tablespoons butter
2 ½ cups chicken broth
¼ cup rice
1 lb. ground beef
¼ cup breadcrumbs
1 whole egg, and 1 egg yolk
¾ teaspoon Italian seasoning
½ teaspoon salt
½ teaspoon pepper
1/8 cup lemon juice

In large pan on stove, cook onions in butter on low setting until soft, about 5 minutes. Add broth, bring to boil, reduce heat and simmer 20 minutes. Meanwhile cook rice according to package directions. In a medium bowl, combine beef, breadcrumbs, whole egg, Italian seasoning, salt, 1/4 teaspoon pepper, and rice. Drop tablespoonfuls into soup and simmer until cooked through. Whisk one egg yolk with lemon juice and ¼ teaspoon pepper. Add some broth to egg mixture, whisk together until smooth and then add to soup pot. Do not reboil. Serve immediately.

Chopped Steak

INGREDIENTS

1 onion, chopped
¼ cup butter
1 lb. ground beef
½ cup flour
1 can tomato paste
¼ cup water
1 tablespoon soy sauce
1 teaspoon salt
1 ½ teaspoon pepper

Sauté onions in butter in large pan over medium heat. Form ground beef into four patties. Dredge patties in flour. Place in skillet with butter and onions. Brown on each side. Add tomato paste, water, soy sauce, salt and pepper to pan, stirring to blend. Simmer for 30 minutes or until cooked through.

Salisbury Steak

INGREDIENTS

1 lb. ground beef
salt and pepper
3 tablespoons flour
2 tablespoons butter
1 can mushrooms, drained
1 onion, sliced
1 ½ cups chicken broth
1 tablespoon Worcestershire sauce

Form beef into four patties. Season with salt and pepper and then coat in flour. In a large pan, heat butter and brown patties on both sides. Add mushrooms and onions to skillet and stir until just warmed. Then add broth, and Worcestershire sauce. Mix through, spooning sauce onto patties. Reduce heat to simmer and cook for additional 25 minutes, stirring occasionally.

35

Soft Shell Tacos

INGREDIENTS

1 lb. ground beef
½ onion, diced
½ cup water
2 tablespoons taco seasoning
1 cup shredded cheddar/jack cheese
1 tomato, diced
1 cup lettuce, shredded
8 tortillas

Brown ground beef with onions. Drain fat. Stir in taco seasoning and water, and cook for an additional 5 minutes. Serve on tortillas and garnish with cheese, tomatoes and lettuce.

Taco Salad

INGREDIENTS

1 lb. ground beef
½ cup water
2 tablespoons taco seasoning
1 cup shredded cheddar/jack cheese
1 head lettuce, chopped
1 tomato, diced
¼ onion, diced
4 tortillas
4 tablespoons oil
Hot Sauce

Form each tortilla on the inside of oven-safe bowl. Weight down with pie weights or dried beans. Brush each with 1 tablespoon oil. Bake at 325° F for 7 minutes each or until crisp. Cool slightly. Meanwhile, brown ground beef with onions. Drain fat. Stir in taco seasoning and water, and cook for an additional 5 minutes. Add equal amounts of lettuce to each tortilla bowl. Top with equal amounts of taco meat and cheese. Garnish with tomatoes, and hot sauce as desired.

Black Bean Tortilla Bake

INGREDIENTS

1 lb. ground beef
2 tablespoons taco seasoning
½ cup water
1 can black beans, drained
1 can diced tomatoes, drained
1 package tortillas

Brown ground beef. Drain. Stir in taco seasoning and water, and cook for an additional 5 minutes. Lay 2 tortillas, overlapping in bottom of a 9 x 13" pan. Add 1/3 ground beef, 1/3 black beans and 1/3 tomatoes. Top with 2 more tortillas, and repeat layering twice. Top with tortillas. Bake, covered, at 350 ° F for 25 minutes. Cut and serve like lasagna.

Beef and Bean Burritos

INGREDIENTS

1 lb. ground beef
½ onion, diced
½ cup water
2 tablespoons taco seasoning
1 cup rice
½ green pepper, finely diced
1 cup chicken broth
2 tablespoons butter
2 tablespoons hot sauce
1 cup shredded cheddar/jack cheese
1 can black beans, rinsed and drained
1 tomato, diced
1 cup shredded lettuce
4 tortillas

Brown ground beef and onion until beef is cooked through. Drain fat. Stir in taco seasoning and water, and cook for an additional 5 minutes. In separate pan, cook rice and green peppers over medium high heat in chicken broth, butter and hot sauce. When rice is nearly done, add beans, stir and continue cooking until rice is done and beans are warm. Place equal portions of beef, beans & rice, cheese, tomatoes and lettuce in each tortilla. Roll and fold in sides to form burritos.

Ground Beef Chili

INGREDIENTS

1 lb. ground beef
1 onion, diced
1 green pepper, diced
salt and pepper to taste
3 tablespoons taco seasoning
1 cup water
1 can diced tomatoes
2 cans black beans, rinsed and drained
1 can tomato paste
hot sauce to taste

Brown ground beef with onion, green pepper, and salt and pepper. Drain fat. Add taco seasoning and water and stir to blend. Add can of tomatoes with juices, black beans, tomato paste and hot sauce as desired. Simmer for at least a half hour until all ingredients set together. Serve over noodles if desired.

Ground Beef Stroganoff

INGREDIENTS

1 can cream of mushroom soup
⅔ cup milk
1 cup bread crumbs
½ onion, finely diced
1 egg
1 lb. ground beef
1 tablespoon Worcestershire sauce
¼ teaspoon salt
¼ teaspoon pepper
1 lb. thick noodles

Preheat oven to 350° F. In large bowl mix soup, milk, bread crumbs, onion, egg, Worcestershire sauce, salt, and pepper until well blended. Add beef and mix well. Spread mixture into 9 inch square baking dish. Bake until lightly browned, about 45 minutes. Meanwhile cook noodles according to package instructions. Serve beef over noodles.

Stuffed Peppers

INGREDIENTS

¾ lb. ground beef
¼ onion, diced
2 cups cooked rice
2 green peppers
1 can diced tomatoes, drained
1 can tomato paste
8 tablespoons honey

In large frying pan cook ground beef and onion until beef is browned.
Drain fat and add rice to beef and onion mix. Cut peppers in half, remove
caps and seeds; rinse. In a separate bowl, mix tomatoes, tomato paste
and honey. Add half tomato/honey mixture to beef and rice and blend.
Add equal portions of beef and rice mixture to each pepper half. Arrange
in baking dish. Top with remaining tomato mixture. Bake, uncovered,
at 350° F for 45 minutes.

* Peppers will still be firm. If you prefer your peppers soft, blanch for
  2 minutes in boiling water.

Fish Recipes

Pecan-Crusted Honey Dijon Fish Fillets

INGREDIENTS

4 fish fillets
2 tablespoons olive oil
2 tablespoons lemon juice
4 teaspoons melted butter
4 teaspoons honey
4 teaspoons Dijon mustard
½ cup crushed pecans

Marinate fish fillets in oil and lemon juice for at least one half hour in refrigerator. Combine mustard, honey and butter. Stir until glaze forms. Discard marinade and place fish in baking pan. Cover with half of glaze, and then pecans. Bake at 375° F for 20 minutes, basting occasionally and at the end with remaining glaze.

Fish Fillets with Lemon Garlic Sauce

INGREDIENTS

4 fish fillets
¼ teaspoon salt
4 tablespoons lemon juice
2 tablespoons butter, softened
1 tablespoon garlic, mashed

Season fish with salt and marinate in 2 tablespoons lemon juice for at least one half hour in refrigerator. Meanwhile with fork, blend butter, garlic and remaining lemon juice. Place fish in baking dish and top with sauce. Bake at 375° F for 20 minutes.

Asian Marinated Fish

INGREDIENTS

4 fish fillets
1 teaspoon lemon juice
⅛ cup soy sauce
½ teaspoon garlic, minced
2 cups mixed vegetables
2 cups rice

Marinate fish in lemon juice and soy sauce for at least one half hour in refrigerator. Wrap each fish fillet loosely in tinfoil tent (raised on all 4 sides to keep juices in). Top each fillet with equal portions of the garlic and the vegetables. Bake at 375° F for 20 minutes. Cook rice according to package directions, and serve fish and vegetables over rice.

Oven Fried Fish

INGREDIENTS

4 tablespoons butter, and ¼ cup melted butter
4 fish fillets
½ teaspoon salt
2 eggs, beaten
⅔ cup flour
1/8 cup water

Spread 4 tablespoons butter in pan, and top with fish. Season fish with salt. Pour eggs over fish and then sprinkle wtih flour. Bake at 350° F for 30 minutes, and baste occasionally with mixture of melted butter and water.

Homestyle Fish Fry

INGREDIENTS

4 fish fillets
4 tablespoons cold water
4 tablespoons salt
2 eggs, separated
2 cups flour
¼ cup oil, and 1 cup oil

Soak fish for 25 minutes in water mixed with 3 tablespoons of salt. Whisk 2 egg yolks and stir in 1 cup flour, water, remaining salt and oil. Beat egg whites until stiff, fold into flour mixture to make batter. Drain fish. Then dip into remaining flour, then into batter, then into flour again and into batter again. Place immediately into hot 1/4 cup oil in deep pan on stove. Fry in oil until golden brown, approximately 8 minutes, turning occasionally.

Cornbread-Crusted Fish with Seasoned Tomatoes

INGREDIENTS

4 fish fillets
1 package cornbread mix
½ onion, diced
1 teaspoon diced garlic
½ green pepper, diced
1 tablespoon olive oil
1 can diced tomatoes
1 teaspoon Italian seasoning
2 cups rice

Dredge fish fillets in cornbread mix. Bake at 350 ° F for 25 minutes or until golden brown. Cook rice according to package directions. Meanwhile, in pan saute onion, garlic and pepper in oil until browned and soft. Add can of tomatoes with about half of the liquid and Italian seasoning, and stir until cooked through. Serve fish on top of tomato mixture with rice.

Parmesan-Crusted Fish Fillets

INGREDIENTS

1 egg, beaten
¼ cup milk
½ cup bread crumbs
2 tablespoons Parmesan cheese
4 fish fillets
¼ teaspoon garlic
¼ cup flour
¼ cup olive oil
1 tablespoon lemon juice

Blend egg and milk. Combine bread crumbs and Parmesan cheese. Rub fish with garlic, then coat with flour. Dip in egg mixture, then dredge in breadcrumb mixture. Fry over medium heat in oil in large skillet for 4-5 minutes per side until fish flakes when tested with a fork. Drain on paper towel and sprinkle with lemon juice.

This fish can also be baked at 350° F for 25 minutes.

Italian Baked Fish with Garlic-Kissed Spinach

INGREDIENTS

¼ cup bread crumbs
1 teaspoon Italian seasoning
¼ teaspoon salt
⅛ teaspoon pepper
½ package frozen spinach, thawed and drained
1 teaspoon garlic, diced
4 tablespoons butter
4 fish fillets

Mix bread crumbs, Italian seasoning, salt and pepper in bowl. In pan on stove, cook thawed spinach with two tablespoons butter and garlic for five minutes until just warmed through. Lay spinach in bottom of baking dish. Dredge fish in two tablespoons melted butter, and then place on top of spinach. Sprinkle bread crumb mixture over fish. Bake at 350° F for 25 minutes.

Cheesy Fish Fillets with Rice

INGREDIENTS

4 fish fillets
2 cups rice
1 cup cheddar/jack cheese
5 tablespoons butter
¾ cup milk
1 tablespoon Dijon mustard
½ cup water
¼ cup bread crumbs

In baking dish, stir together rice, milk, mustard, water, three tablespoons butter and ½ cup cheddar/jack cheese. Top with fish. Bake at 375° F for 15 minutes. Remove from oven, top with remaining cheese, bread crumbs and sprinkle with 2 tablespoons butter, melted. Bake for 10 minutes more or until lightly browned.

Fish Florentine

INGREDIENTS

4 fish fillets
salt and pepper
¼ cup onion, diced
½ teaspoon Italian seasoning
2 tablespoons butter
1 package frozen spinach, drained and thawed
1 cup rice, cooked
1 tablespoon lemon juice
1 can cream of mushroom soup
¼ cup water

Season fish with salt and pepper to taste. In saucepan, cook onion with Italian seasoning in butter until tender. Add spinach, rice and lemon juice to pan and cook, stirring occassionally for 8 minutes. Place fish fillets in a baking dish. Top each fillet with 1/4 rice mixture. Bake, uncovered, at 350° F for 20 minutes. Blend soup and water. Pour over fish. Return to oven and bake for 10 minutes.

Pizza Recipes

Who knew homemade pizza dough could be so delicious and easy? It can also be made a day in advance, and quantities can be doubled, or tripled and frozen for future use.

Pizza crust

INGREDIENTS

1 ¼ cups flour
½ packet (1/8 oz.) dry yeast
½ teaspoon salt
½ cup very warm water (120-130 degrees)
1 tablespoon vegetable oil

Generously grease a baking sheet, and place on middle rack of oven. In a medium bowl, stir together 1/2 cup of the flour, yeast and salt until well blended. Add water and oil. Mix until almost smooth. Gradually stir in remaining flour to make a firm dough. Cover; let set for 15 minutes. Generously prick dough with fork. Roll out and prebake at 400° F for 10 to 12 minutes or just until edges of crust begin to turn a light golden brown. Remove from oven.

Traditional Homemade Pizza

INGREDIENTS

Pizza Crust (see recipe on p. 75)
1 can diced tomatoes, mostly drained
1 can tomato paste
½ teaspoon garlic salt
1 teaspoon Italian seasoning
1 ½ cups shredded Mozzarella cheese
Toppings of your choice

Mix together tomatoes and tomato paste. Spread on pizza crust, top with garlic salt and Italian seasoning, additional toppings of your choice, if desired, and cheese. Bake on a hot baking sheet in a 400° F oven for 15 minutes or until golden brown.

Barbecue Chicken Pizza

INGREDIENTS

Pizza Crust (see recipe on p. 75)
½ onion, sliced
2 chicken breasts, diced
1 tablespoon butter
1 teaspoon sugar
1 cup barbecue sauce (see recipe below)
1 green pepper, sliced
1 cup shredded Mozzarella cheese

BARBECUE SAUCE

1 can tomato paste
¼ onion, chopped
2 teaspoons sugar
1 tablespoon Dijon mustard
1 teaspoon soy sauce
1 teaspoon garlic salt
1 teaspoon hot sauce

For barbecue sauce, combine tomato paste, onion, sugar, mustard, soy sauce, garlic salt and hot sauce in pan. Stir well and cook 2 minutes over medium heat until onion is tender. Keep warm.

Meanwhile, cook onions and chicken in butter in large frying pan over medium-high heat until cooked through, stirring frequently. Stir in 1 teaspoon sugar; cook until melted. Keep warm. Spread barbecue sauce on pizza, top with chicken, peppers, onions and cheese. Bake on a hot baking sheet in a 400° F oven for 15 minutes or until golden brown.

Spinach and Mushroom Pizza

INGREDIENTS

Pizza Crust (see recipe on p.75)
½ teaspoon diced garlic
1 can mushrooms, drained
1 tablespoon butter
1 can diced tomatoes, drained
1 can tomato paste
½ package frozen spinach, thawed
1 ½ cups shredded mozzarella cheese

In a small pan on stove, saute garlic and mushrooms in butter for three minutes. Top pizza crust with tomato paste, tomatoes, spinach, and mushroom/garlic mixture. Sprinkle with cheese, and bake at 400° F for 15 minutes or until golden brown.

Mexican Pizza

INGREDIENTS

Pizza Crust (see recipe on p.75)
½ lb. ground beef
½ onion, diced
3 teaspoons taco seasoning
¼ cup water
1 can diced tomatoes, mostly drained
1 can tomato paste
⅔ cup shredded cheddar cheese
½ green pepper, diced
¾ cup shredded lettuce, optional

Brown ground beef with onion. Drain fat. Add water and taco seasoning and cook over low heat an additional 5 minutes or until most of the liquid evaporates. Remove from heat. Add tomatoes. Spread tomato paste on crust. Top with beef and tomatoes, peppers and cheese. Bake at 400° F for 15 minutes or until golden brown. Top with shredded lettuce just before serving, if desired.

Pasta, Soups & More

Easy Chicken Fettuccine

INGREDIENTS

1 lb. thick pasta noodles
½ cup butter
4 chicken breasts, diced
2 tablespoons diced garlic
¼ onion, chopped
2 cups milk
1 ½ cups Parmesan cheese
1 teaspoon Italian seasoning
1 teaspoon salt
1 teaspoon pepper
1 tablespoon lemon juice

Cook pasta according to package directions. Melt butter in skillet and saute chicken with garlic and onions, for 5 minutes. Add remaining ingredients except lemon juice, cover and simmer over low heat until mixture thickens and chicken is tender, stirring often. Add pasta to pan and mix through. Sprinkle with lemon juice and additional Parmesan cheese.

Chicken Artichoke Mushroom Pasta Fiesta

INGREDIENTS

2 chicken breasts, cut into strips
½ teaspoon Italian seasoning
salt and pepper to taste
3 tablespoons olive oil
3 tablespoons diced onion
1 teaspoon diced garlic
1 can sliced mushrooms
1 can marinated artichokes
1 tablespoon balsamic vinegar
1 can diced tomatoes
1 lb. macaroni or other thick pasta noodles
⅓ cup Parmesan Cheese

Season chicken with Italian seasoning, salt and pepper. Cook chicken in oil in frying pan over medium heat. When nearly cooked through, add onions, garlic, mushrooms, artichokes with a little juice, and balsamic vinegar. Stir constantly until blended and warmed, about 4 minutes. Add tomatoes with some of their juices. Meanwhile, cook pasta according to package directions. Stir chicken mixture immediately into pasta. Serve with Parmesan cheese.

Baked Pasta

INGREDIENTS

8 oz. thick pasta
1 medium onion, chopped
2 tablespoons minced garlic
1 can diced tomatoes
1 can tomato paste
2 teaspoons Italian seasoning
1 teaspoon garlic salt
½ teaspoon hot sauce
2 cups Mozzarella cheese
½ cup Parmesan cheese
¼ cup water
½ package frozen spinach, thawed and drained

Cook pasta according to al dente package directions, drain and return to pot. In a large skillet, cook onion and garlic over medium heat until lightly browned, about 5 minutes. Stir in tomatoes, tomato paste, Italian seasoning, salt and hot sauce. Stir vigorously and simmer 5 minutes. Add noodles, water, sauce, spinach and 1 ½ cups Mozzarella cheese to a large baking dish. Stir to blend. Cover with remaining ½ cup Mozzarella and Parmesan cheese and bake 30 – 40 minutes, covered, at 325° F until bubbly. Remove foil toward the end if you would like cheese browned on top.

Southwest Pasta

INGREDIENTS

2 chicken breasts, diced
2 tablespoons olive oil
1 teaspoon lemon juice
2 teaspoons Taco seasoning
8 oz. thick pasta
½ green pepper, diced
¼ onion, diced
1 can black beans, drained and rinsed
2 teaspoons hot sauce
1 can diced tomatoes

Marinate chicken in oil, lemon juice and taco seasoning for one half hour. Cook pasta according to package directions. Cook chicken in a pan on stove over medium heat, until just browned. Add pepper and onion and cook a few minutes more. Stir in black beans, hot sauce and tomatoes and continue cooking for 10 more minutes until chicken is cooked through, and flavors are blended. Remove from heat. Blend with pasta and serve.

Pasta Bolognese

INGREDIENTS

½ lb. ground beef
8 oz. pasta
½ tablespoon garlic, diced
3 tablespoons diced onion
1 tablespoon balsamic vinegar
salt and pepper to taste
2 tablespoons olive oil
1 can diced tomatoes
1 can tomato paste
1 tablespoon hot sauce
½ cup water
1 teaspoon honey
1 cup Mozzarella cheese
¼ cup Parmesan cheese

Brown ground beef in pan on stove with onions and garlic until no longer pink. Drain fat. Add vinegar, salt and pepper, tomatoes, tomato paste, hot sauce, and honey to pan and continue to cook, stirring frequently, 10 minutes. To baking dish, add pasta, water, meat sauce and Mozzarella cheese. Stir until blended. Bake at 350° F for 45 minutes. Top with Parmesan cheese and serve.

61

Asian Noodle Bake

INGREDIENTS

2 chicken breasts, diced
8 oz. uncooked pasta
1 cup uncooked rice
2 cups chicken broth
¼ cup soy sauce
1 teaspoon minced garlic
5 tablespoons butter
2 tablespoons Worcestershire sauce
½ cup water

Sear chicken in 1 tablespoon of the butter in pan on stove until just browned. Put pasta and rice in a large baking dish. Stir in remaining ingredients including chicken. Cover and bake at 350° F for 1 hour.

62

Italian Vegetable Soup

INGREDIENTS

½ package frozen spinach, thawed and drained
1 tomato, diced, OR 1 can diced tomatoes, drained
1 can mushrooms, drained
½ onion, diced
2 tablespoons olive oil
1 teaspoon garlic, minced
1 teaspoon Italian seasoning
4 cups chicken broth
1 cup small noodles, or broken spaghetti noodles

Cook spinach, tomatoes, mushrooms, onion and garlic in olive oil on stove for 10 minutes until lightly browned. Season vegetables with Italian seasoning, and add to stock pot. Add broth, and bring to a boil. Reduce heat and simmer for 20 minutes. Add pasta and simmer for an additional 10 minutes.

63

Tomato Florentine Soup

INGREDIENTS

2 tablespoons butter
2 tablespoons flour
1 teaspoon garlic salt
½ teaspoon black pepper
2 cans diced tomatoes
14 oz. chicken broth
1 cup milk or cream
⅓ package frozen spinach, thawed and drained
⅓ cup Parmesan cheese

Add first four ingredients to medium pot and heat on stove over medium heat, stirring frequently until bubbly. Add tomatoes and broth, and simmer for at least 25 minutes. Stir in remaining ingredients, blend if deisred, and serve.

Black Bean Soup

INGREDIENTS

½ lb. ground beef
1 onion, diced
2 tablespoons garlic, diced
½ green pepper, diced
2 cups chicken broth
2 cans black beans, drained and rinsed
1 can diced tomatoes
2 tablespoons Hot sauce
1 tablespoon lemon juice

Brown ground beef with onion, garlic and green pepper until cooked through. Drain fat. Add to stock pot with chicken broth, black beans and tomatoes. Bring to a boil and then reduce heat to medium low. Add hot sauce and lemon juice, and simmer uncovered for 45 minutes. Stir frequently.

Chicken Noodle Soup

INGREDIENTS

2 tablespoons butter
¼ onion, diced
2 tablespoons flour
4 cups chicken broth
2 chicken breasts, diced
1 cup frozen mixed vegetables, thawed
1 cup dry pasta
salt

Brown onion in butter in stock pot on stove. Add flour and stir until thick and bubbly. Stir in broth. Add chicken and bring to a boil. Reduce heat and simmer about 40 minutes. Add vegetables and pasta, and simmer for an additional 20 minutes. Add salt to taste.

Tamale Pie

INGREDIENTS

1 can black beans, drained and rinsed
1 can diced tomatoes, drained
½ onion, diced
½ green pepper, diced
1 package cornbread mix

Add black beans, diced tomatoes, onions and peppers to 8 x 8" or 9 x 9" baking dish. Prepare cornbread mixture, according to package directions, and pour over top. Bake at 400° for 20 minutes. Remove from oven and let sit 10 minutes before serving.

Simple Spinach Quiche

Quiche is another versatile dish. If you prefer different
vegetables, they can easily be substituted for the spinach.

INGREDIENTS

1 pie crust
3 eggs
1 cup milk
½ package frozen spinach
2 tablespoons butter
¼ onion, chopped
½ teaspoon garlic salt
1 cup cheddar/jack cheese
½ cup Parmesan cheese
¼ teaspoon pepper

Place pie crust in pie plate. Prick with a fork, and bake at 375° F for 9 minutes.
Beat eggs and milk. Cook spinach with onions, butter, 2 tablespoons water,
and garlic salt, until just cooked through. Drain excess liquid and spoon onto
pie crust. Top with both cheeses and egg mixture. Sprinkle with pepper. Bake
at 375° F for 25 minutes or until top is firm.

Tomato Artichoke Quiche

INGREDIENTS

1 pie crust
3 eggs
1 cup milk
½ teaspoon salt
¼ teaspoon pepper
1 can diced tomatoes, drained, or 1 fresh tomato, sliced
1 jar marinated artichokes, drained
1 cup cheddar/jack cheese
¼ onion, chopped

Place pie crust in pie plate. Prick with a fork, and bake at 375° F for 9 minutes. Beat eggs and milk. Add salt and pepper. Add tomatoes and artichokes to pie crust. Top with cheese, onions, and egg mixture. Bake at 375° F for 25 minutes or until top is firm.

Spinach and Cheese Enchiladas

INGREDIENTS

1 can tomato paste
3 tablespoons vegetable oil
2 teaspoons taco seasoning
1 teaspoon hot sauce
2 teaspoons flour
1 cup water
1 teaspoon garlic salt
2 tablespoons butter
1 package frozen spinach, thawed and drained
1 tablespoon diced garlic
½ onion, diced
1 tomato, diced, or 1 can diced tomatoes, drained
2 cups shredded cheddar/jack cheese
8 tortillas

For sauce, combine tomato paste, oil, taco seasoning, hot sauce, flour, water and garlic salt in pan on stove. Bring to boil; simmer 5 minutes.

Heat oven to 425° F. In a small pan on stove, warm butter over medium heat. Add spinach, garlic and onions. Stir until warmed through. Remove from heat and stir in tomatoes. Using 1 cup cheese, and all spinach mixture, place small handfuls of each in center of each tortilla, roll up and place in pan, seam side down. Sprinkle with remaining cheese. Ladle on enough sauce to cover, then add remaining 1/4 cup cheese. Bake 20 minutes. Serve with remaining sauce on the side.

Vegetable Frittata

INGREDIENTS

2 cups cooked pasta
4 eggs
¼ cup milk
½ cup frozen spinach, thawed and drained
1 green pepper, diced
1 tomato, diced
½ cup pepper/jack cheese
1 teaspoon Italian seasoning
1 teaspoon salt
½ teaspoon pepper
2 tablespoons olive oil

Coat bottom and sides of baking dish with olive oil. Mix all ingredients in large bowl and pour into casserole dish. Bake at 375° F for 30 minutes.

Side Dish Suggestions

Many of the 70 meals in this book include rice or pasta and therefore don't need a side dish. For those that don't here are some quick and easy side dish recipes that (of course) use only ingredients on your Semiannual and Weekly Lists.

Rice Pilaf

INGREDIENTS

4 tablespoons butter
¼ green pepper, finely diced
¼ onion, finely diced
1 ½ cups rice, uncooked
14 oz. chicken broth
¼ cup water

Melt butter in large pan on stove. Add vegetables and stir until just cooked through, about 5 minutes. Add rice, broth and water. Bring to a boil. Reduce heat and simmer until liquid is absorbed.

Mexican Rice

INGREDIENTS

1 can diced tomatoes
1 ½ cups uncooked rice
1 teaspoon taco seasoning
1 tablespoon butter
½ cup water
½ cup chicken broth

Add all ingredients to pot on stove. Bring to a boil. Reduce heat and simmer until liquid is absorbed.

Buttered Noodles

INGREDIENTS

1 ½ cups pasta
¼ cup butter
¼ cup Parmesan cheese

Cook pasta according to package directions. Drain. Add butter to hot pasta and stir through. Stir in Parmesan cheese.

Noodles with Vegetables

INGREDIENTS

1 ½ cups uncooked pasta
⅛ cup butter
½ cups Parmesan cheese
¼ onion, chopped
½ teaspoon garlic salt
½ teaspoon pepper
1 cup frozen vegetables, thawed

Cook pasta according to package directions. Melt butter in skillet. Add onions and stir until just cooked through. Add cooked pasta, vegetables, garlic salt and pepper to the pan and stir through. Top with Parmesan cheese.

70
MEALS
one
TRIP TO THE STORE

To order additional copies of
70 Meals, One Trip to the Store
and learn about our other cookbooks,
cooking classes and upcoming events,
visit our website at
www.organizingdinner.com.

KELLYOONLEA